SPORTS
DYNASTIES

DEREK JETER

AND THE NEW YORK YANKEES

abdopublishing.com

Published by Abdo Publishing, a division of ABDO, PO Box 398166, Minneapolis, Minnesota 55439.
Copyright © 2019 by Abdo Consulting Group, Inc. International copyrights reserved in all countries.
No part of this book may be reproduced in any form without written permission from the publisher.
SportsZone™ is a trademark and logo of Abdo Publishing.

Printed in the United States of America, North Mankato, Minnesota
052018
092018

Cover Photos: John Froschauer/AP Images, left; Charles Krupa/AP Images, right
Interior Photos: Kathy Willens/AP Images, 4–5; John Bazemore/AP Images, 7, 9; Adam Nadel/AP Images,
10; Richard Harbus/AP Images, 12–13; Diamond Images/Getty Images, 14; Tyler Bolden/MJA/Four Seam
Images/AP Images, 17; Ken Babbitt/Four Seam Images/AP Images, 18; Paul Warner/AP Images, 20–21;
David Dermer/Diamond Images/Getty Images, 22; Louis Lopez/Cal Sport Media/AP Images, 25; Ron
Frehm/AP Images, 26; Duane Burleson/AP Images, 29; Jack Balletti UPI Photo Service/Newscom, 30–31;
Brad Mangin/Sports Illustrated/Getty Images, 32; Frank Franklin II/AP Images, 35; Roberto Borea/
AP Images, 36; Chris O'Meara/AP Images, 38–39; Mike Janes/Four Seam Images/AP Images, 40;
Willie J. Allen Jr./AP Images, 43

Editor: Bradley Cole
Series Designer: Craig Hinton

Library of Congress Control Number: 2017962577

Publisher's Cataloging-in-Publication Data

Names: Karpovich, Todd, author.
Title: Derek Jeter and the New York Yankees / by Todd Karpovich.
Description: Minneapolis, Minnesota : Abdo Publishing, 2019. | Series: Sports dynasties | Includes online
    resources and index.
Identifiers: ISBN 9781532114328 (lib.bdg.) | ISBN 9781532154157 (ebook)
Subjects: LCSH: Jeter, Derek, 1974-.--Juvenile literature. | Baseball players--United States--Biography-
    -Juvenile literature. | Baseball--Juvenile literature. | New York Yankees (Baseball team)--Juvenile
    literature.
Classification: DDC 796.357092 [B]--dc23

TABLE OF CONTENTS

CHAPTER 1

THE
EARLY DAYS

D erek Jeter didn't take long to prove that he was one of the best shortstops and best players in the world. In New York City, the New York Yankees trailed the Baltimore Orioles 4–3. It was the eighth inning of Game 1 of the 1996 American League Championship Series (ALCS). The Yankees desperately needed a spark. Their rookie shortstop was up to the task.

Jeter hit a long fly ball to right field. Orioles outfielder Tony Tarasco settled under the

Derek Jeter provided a much-needed spark for the Yankees in the 1996 ALCS.

ball, ready to catch it just short of the fence. But a 12-year-old
Yankees fan reached over and caught the ball. The Orioles
argued it was fan interference, but the umpires ruled it a home
run. New York would go on to win that game 5–4.

The Orioles never recovered in the series. New York beat
Baltimore four games to one. Jeter hit a home run and two
doubles and scored five runs in the series.

Next up were the Atlanta Braves, who were the defending
World Series champions. The Braves were a veteran team.
Their core players had reached the World Series for the fourth
time in the past six seasons. New York was playing in its first
World Series since 1981. The Yankees, though, had an exciting
group of young players, led by Jeter.

DIVISION RIVALS

The 1996 ALCS was far from the last time that Derek Jeter would torment the
Orioles. In almost 300 career games against the Orioles, Jeter hit .296, scored
206 runs, and drove in 144 more. But on September 14, 2014, when he played
his last game at Baltimore's Camden Yards, Orioles fans gave him an extended
standing ovation.

JETER'S FIRST WORLD SERIES

The 1996 World Series did not start well for the Yankees. They lost the opening two games at home by a combined score of 16–1. But the Yankees did not lose their confidence. New York bounced back in Atlanta with a 5–2 victory. Game 4 would change the entire momentum of the series.

The Yankees were behind 6–0 by the fifth inning. New York began to chip away with three runs in the sixth and then tied the score in the eighth. The game went to extra innings. The tension at the stadium could be felt even on the TV broadcast.

In the 10th inning, the Yankees started to rally with two outs. Braves reliever Steve Avery walked Tim Raines and then allowed a single by Jeter. Avery then intentionally walked Bernie Williams to load the bases. This would allow an out at any base on the following play. But Wade Boggs drew a walk that put New York ahead 7–6. Charlie Hayes followed with a short pop-up that dropped safely between the Braves fielders, allowing Jeter to score. The Yankees hung on to win 8–6. This was the second-biggest comeback in World Series history.

New York won the fifth game of the series 1–0 behind a masterful performance by ace pitcher Andy Pettitte.

Yankees ace pitcher Jimmy Key was vital in winning Game 6 of the 1996 World Series, which started the Yankees dynasty.

The Yankees were able to return home for Game 6 and play in front of a sold-out crowd. They got all the runs they would need with a three-run third inning. Once again Jeter was a catalyst for the rally as he singled home a run, stole a base, and scored.

The 1996 Yankees celebrated their first World Series in 18 years.

Yankees closer John Wetteland got Atlanta's Mark Lemke to hit a pop-up in foul territory for the final out in the 3–2 victory. It set off a wild celebration in the Bronx. The Yankees had clinched their first World Series championship since 1978. It was their 23rd world title in franchise history. Wetteland saved all four New York victories and was named the World Series Most Valuable Player (MVP).

THE BEGINNING OF A DYNASTY

This was the beginning of a dynasty. Under the guidance of manager Joe Torre, the Yankees won the World Series three more times over the next four years (1998, 1999, and 2000). Jeter led the charge as a young shortstop who managed to improve each season. Torre's gamble to name Jeter as the team's starting shortstop just prior to the 1996 season proved to be a wise decision. That first World Series win was just the beginning of Jeter's storied career. Jeter went on to become one of the greatest shortstops of all time. His success was the culmination of a lifetime of hard work and support from his teammates.

CHAPTER 2

DEVELOPMENT

Derek Jeter was born in Pequannock, New Jersey, not far from Yankee Stadium. Jeter's family moved to Kalamazoo, Michigan when he was four. Jeter was always a good athlete, and he played both basketball and baseball at Kalamazoo Central High School. This is also where his dreams of playing professional baseball started to become a reality.

Jeter batted over .500 in both his junior and senior years, and during his senior year he struck

Jeter, *left*, meets with Yankees players Jim Leyritz and Mike Gallego a few months after the 1992 MLB Draft.

Jeter was sent to the Gulf Coast Rookie League after his first spring training with the Yankees.

out just once all season. As a result, he was named the national player of the year by the American High School Coaches Association, Gatorade, and *USA Today*.

Jeter didn't have to wait long to begin his journey as a professional baseball player. Shortly after graduating from high school in 1992, he was chosen sixth overall by the New York Yankees in the Major League Baseball (MLB) draft. Drafting a high school position player can be a gamble for a major league team. Because the talent of high school pitchers can vary so much, it's often difficult to predict how a young batter will fare against professional pitching. The Yankees, however, were rewarded for their decision.

Jeter steadily climbed in the Yankees' minor league system. Shortly after being drafted, he was assigned to the Gulf Coast Rookie League. He initially struggled and batted just .202 over 47 games. For a player used to batting over .500, that could have shaken his confidence. Instead Jeter stayed determined and worked hard to get better. He was rewarded with a late-season call-up to Class-A Greensboro, where he played well in an 11-game stint.

In 1993 he began at Greensboro, still four steps away from the major leagues. He played much better than he did the year before. The Yankees were not surprised. They were confident he would get better. However, their young short stop committed

56 errors as he adjusted to playing baseball every day for the first time in his life. He worked all winter to address his weaknesses on the field.

CLIMBING THROUGH THE MINOR LEAGUES

Jeter's breakout season came in 1994 when he was promoted twice during the season. He began the year Class A-Advanced Tampa, one step higher than Greensboro. The Yankees bumped him up to Double-A Albany when his success continued against better pitchers. Jeter stayed there for just 34 games. A promotion to the Triple-A Columbus team left him just one step from the big leagues. He finished the season by hitting .349 over 35 games at Columbus. Perhaps even better, in 138 games between three levels he committed just 25 errors.

After the season, Jeter was named the minor league player of the year by both *The Sporting News* and *Baseball America*. Jeter was also ranked as the No. 2 prospect in baseball, right behind future teammate Alex Rodriguez. More important, the Yankees were confident Jeter was almost ready to perform at the major league level.

Jeter returned to Triple-A Columbus for the beginning of the 1995 season, and he did not slow down. The Yankees

Jeter played in the minor leagues from 1993 through the beginning of the 1996 season.

closely monitored his progress. Then Yankees starting shortstop Tony Fernandez was forced to the disabled list with a pulled muscle in his rib cage. On May 29, 1995, Jeter was promoted to the major leagues.

Jeter impressed the Yankees with his hitting as he climbed through the minor leagues.

Jeter was hitless in five at-bats in his debut. But he showed his resilience the following night as he picked up his first major league hit off Mariners pitcher Tim Belcher. Over the course of the next two weeks, Jeter started every game. He had at least one hit in 9 of 13 games and committed two errors. The Yankees believed they had found their long-term answer at shortstop. But they did not want to rush him. When Fernandez was healthy, Jeter was sent back to Columbus to finish his development. The next time he was called up, it would be on a one-way ticket to New York.

DURABILITY

One of the keys for Derek Jeter's career was his ability to stay healthy. Jeter was a mainstay in the lineup. He played in 2,747 games over his 20 years as a Yankee. Jeter did suffer a major injury in 2003. He had a separated shoulder after an on-field collision. Jeter missed 39 games, but he returned and was as good as ever. The injury kept him out of the All-Star game. Jeter earned those honors again the following year. He also missed most of the 2013 season due to injuries. He appeared in only 17 games that season.

CHAPTER 3

KEY FIGURES

While Jeter was a natural leader and an example to young players with his strong work ethic, he had several major influences throughout his career. Several teammates and managers helped shape him into a Hall of Fame–caliber player.

In 1996 the Yankees hired Joe Torre as manager. Torre was a talented catcher and third baseman in his playing days. But he'd had mixed success in three prior stops managing the

Joe Torre, *left*, was instrumental to Derek Jeter's development and the resurgence of the Yankees.

New York Mets, the Atlanta Braves, and the St. Louis Cardinals. In fact the Cardinals fired Torre 47 games into the 1995 season. It seems incredible now, given the success he went on to have, but when the Yankees hired Torre, he was seen as anything but a sure thing.

Torre's first bold move was naming the 21-year-old Jeter his starting shortstop. Jeter responded by batting .314 with 10 home runs and 78 runs batted in (RBIs) over 157 games, officially his first full season as a major leaguer. His strong play earned him the American League (AL) Rookie of the Year Award.

Jeter's productivity was typical of a Yankees player under Torre. In the 12 seasons with Torre as the Yankees' manager, his teams won the AL East Division 10 times. And they made the playoffs as a wild card the other two years. Torre was lauded for his even-keel approach to the game. He was a calming influence who worked well with veterans and young players. For the Yankees, he was the right manager at the right time.

When Torre moved on, he was replaced by a familiar face. Joe Girardi had been a catcher for the New York Yankees from

1996 to 1999. His experience and leadership made him a great manager. Girardi took over from Torre in 2007, and two years later, he led the Yankees to their 27th World Series title.

PITCHING PROS

From Whitey Ford in the 1950s and '60s to Ron Guidry in the 1970s and '80s, the best Yankees teams have been anchored by an elite left-handed pitcher. Andy Pettitte filled that role for the Jeter-led dynasty.

Pettitte pitched for the Yankees from 1995 to 2003 and from 2007 to 2013. In his second year with the team, he led the AL with 21 victories as the Yankees began their World Series run. In 1997 Pettitte was named the Yankees' Opening Day starter. Pettitte was never a big strikeout pitcher. But he was a durable pitcher who rarely missed his turn in the rotation and was reliable in the biggest games. He won two games in the Yankees' 2009 World Series victory over Philadelphia, and his 19 postseason wins are the most in MLB history.

When Pettitte or any of his fellow starters tired, they usually could rely on a dominant bullpen to finish things off.

For most of the Yankees' dynasty that bullpen was anchored by Mariano Rivera. The 13-time All-Star pitched for the Yankees from 1995 to 2013. He dominated his opponents even though they usually knew what was coming. Rivera relied on a "cutter," or cut fastball. The pitch's late movement broke away from right-handed hitters and toward lefties. It was virtually unhittable. He retired with a record 652 career saves, a mark that will be hard to beat.

SUPER SLUGGERS

The 1990s championship teams relied on valuable contributions from a number of experienced position players. Third baseman Scott Brosius, first baseman Tino Martinez, and right fielder Paul O'Neill were among these veterans. They set the pace for Jeter and two other key figures who would themselves become veteran leaders of championship teams.

Jorge Posada became the Yankees' regular catcher in 1998 and helped them win three straight World Series. A switch hitter with power, Posada was a five-time winner of the Silver Slugger

Award, given to the league's best hitter at each position. He played his entire career with the Yankees, retiring in 2011.

Along with Posada and Jeter, center fielder Bernie Williams was a constant presence in the Yankees lineup through most of their glory years. Williams was already 27 and a three-year starter when the Yankees made their World Series run in 1996. But he blossomed when he entered his prime that year. Williams drove in at least 100 runs in five of the next seven years. He covered center field as well, winning four straight Gold Glove Awards from 1997 to 2000. He retired in 2006, three years before Jeter would lead the Yankees to one final championship.

JETER'S LAST WORLD SERIES

Derek Jeter celebrated his last World Series title in 2009. The Yankees were the heavy favorite after finishing the regular season with the most wins in the league at 103–59. The Yankees then trailed in all three of their AL Division Series (ALDS) games against the Minnesota Twins, but they still managed a sweep. New York then advanced to the World Series and beat the Philadelphia Phillies in six games for its 27th title. Jeter batted an astounding .407 with three doubles. Despite those gaudy numbers, teammate Hideki Matsui took home MVP honors. Matsui tied an MLB record with six RBIs in the final game of the series.

CHAPTER 4

HIGHLIGHTS

During a crisp October night, fans at the Oakland Coliseum watched one of the greatest plays in baseball history. It was Game 3 of the 2001 ALDS between the Oakland Athletics and the New York Yankees. New York had lost the first two games at home. Facing elimination back in Oakland, the Yankees clung to a 1–0 lead with two outs in the seventh inning. With a runner on first, the Athletics' Terrence Long came to the plate, looking to tie the game.

Tino Martinez, *right*, scores the only run of Game 3 of the 2001 ALDS.

Long scorched a line drive down the right-field line. The ball rolled toward the fence. Oakland's Jeremy Giambi got a good jump off first base and began to round the bases.

Right fielder Shane Spencer scooped up the ball and hurled it toward the infield. He overthrew two teammates who were in line to cut off the ball and relay it home. Giambi touched third base and headed toward home plate. It appeared that he would score easily.

Instead, Jeter had raced from short stop across to the right side of the diamond and scooped up the errant relay throw. His momentum was carrying him across the first base line about halfway between home and first. But in one motion Jeter caught the ball and flipped it backhanded to Jorge Posada. The Yankees catcher tagged Giambi just before he crossed the plate. The Yankees players streamed from the dugout to celebrate Jeter's amazing play.

It became known as "the Flip." The play changed the entire series. The Yankees held on to win 1–0. The stunned A's never recovered. Two games later the Yankees won the series. Those were the types of plays that defined Jeter's career.

THE DIVE

One of Jeter's most famous catches is known as "the Dive." Jeter flew into the stands face-first to catch a foul ball against the Boston Red Sox in 2004. The Yankee Stadium crowd roared when Jeter came up with the ball. Several teammates rushed to the third base side of the field as several security officers pulled Jeter from the stands.

Jeter played key roles in each of the Yankees' World Series wins. He hit a home run on the first pitch of Game 4 against the New York Mets in 2000. His homer zapped the energy from

THE SUBWAY SERIES

The "Subway Series" between the Yankees and the Mets in 2000 was one of the most highly anticipated World Series in the history of baseball. The crosstown rivals are separated by about 7 miles (11 km). It was also the first time two New York teams faced off for a World Series title since 1956. But the series itself was a bit anticlimactic. The Yankees dominated from the start and won four games to one.

Jeter dives into the stands to make a catch against the rival Boston Red Sox.

the Mets, and the home crowd went silent. The Yankees never trailed in a 3–2 victory. They won the title with a 4–2 victory in Game 5.

Jeter also hit a game-winning home run in the 10th inning of Game 4 of the 2001 World Series. The homer off

Arizona Diamondbacks reliever Byung-Hyun Kim tied the series at two games apiece. Jeter's homer came shortly after midnight on November 1. The scoreboard at Yankee Stadium flashed a sign that read "Welcome to November Baseball." Jeter would later earn the nickname "Mr. November," a play on the nickname of former Yankees star Reggie Jackson, who was known as "Mr. October."

Jeter finished his career with many Yankees records. He is the club's all-time leader in games played, at-bats, hits, doubles, hit by pitches, strikeouts, and stolen bases. His career at Yankee Stadium came to an end on September 25, 2014. In his final at-bat, Jeter hit a game-winning single. The hit set off a wild party among the New York fans.

CHAPTER 5

ROSTER CHANGES

When Jeter decided to retire as a player, many of his former managers, teammates, and fans believed he would remain involved with the game in some capacity. Jeter was a baseball icon and had a lot to offer as a coach, manager, or front office executive.

Jeter's absence not only left a void in the game. It left a huge hole in the Yankees lineup. Before the 2015 season, they traded for

Jeter retired from baseball after 20 seasons with the Yankees.

25-year-old Arizona Diamondbacks shortstop Didi Gregorius. He took over as the starting shortstop and held his own despite having such big shoes to fill.

Meanwhile Jeter continued to put his stamp on the game. In October 2017, he was part of a group that announced an agreement to buy the Miami Marlins for $1.2 billion. Jeter reportedly owns 4 percent of the team and serves as its chief executive officer.

Outside of baseball, Jeter remains highly regarded for his charity work with the Turn 2 Foundation. The organization helps children and teenagers avoid drug and alcohol addiction. He also started a website called the *Players Tribune*. It allows professional athletes to share first-person stories about their experiences and concerns.

ASSEMBLING THE FUTURE

The Yankees moved on from the Jeter era and got to work assembling their next great team. Hard-hitting outfielder Aaron Judge was named the 2017 AL Rookie of the Year after he blasted 52 home runs. And before the 2018 season began, they made a trade with Jeter's new team, landing slugger Giancarlo Stanton, who led the majors with 59 home runs the year before. Yankees fans dreamed of watching Judge and Stanton send baseballs into orbit for many summers to come.

New York parted ways with manager Joe Girardi after the 2017 season. They hired another former Yankee, Aaron Boone, to replace him. Boone's claim to fame was hitting an 11th-inning home run against the Red Sox in Game 7 of the 2003 ALCS to put the Yankees into the World Series. He hoped to build off the momentum of New York's run to the ALCS in 2017.

JOE TORRE

When he retired as a manager, Joe Torre was a perfect fit to help run Major League Baseball. He was named Executive Vice President for Baseball Operations in February 2011. Torre also was named manager of the US team in the 2013 World Baseball Classic. He was inducted into the National Baseball Hall of Fame in 2014.

NEW YORK YANKEES

SPAN OF DYNASTY

- 1996 through 2014

WORLD SERIES WON

- 5 (1996, 1998, 1999, 2000, 2009)

AL EAST TITLES

- 13 (1996, 1998, 1999, 2000, 2001, 2002, 2003, 2004, 2005, 2006, 2009, 2011, 2012)

REGULAR SEASON RECORD

1,821–1,253

PLAYOFF RECORD

97–64

KEY RIVALS

- Boston Red Sox
- New York Mets
- Cleveland Indians
- Atlanta Braves

INDIVIDUAL AWARDS

MLB MVP

Alex Rodriguez (2003, 2005, 2007)

AL MANAGER OF THE YEAR

Joe Torre (1996, 1998)

CY YOUNG

Roger Clemens (2001)

WORLD SERIES MVP

- John Wetteland (1996)
- Scott Brosius (1998)
- Mariano Rivera (1999)
- Derek Jeter (2000)
- Hideki Matsui (2009)

DEREK JETER HONORS

- All-Star appearances: 14
- AL Rookie of the Year: 1996
- World Series MVP: 2000
- Golden Glove: 2004, 2005, 2006, 2009, 2010

JUNE 1, 1992

The Yankees select Jeter sixth overall in the 1992 MLB draft.

MAY 29, 1995

Jeter makes his MLB debut.

OCTOBER 26, 1996

The Yankees beat the Atlanta Braves in the World Series.

NOVEMBER 5, 1996

Jeter is named AL Rookie of the Year.

OCTOBER 21, 1998

The Yankees sweep the San Diego Padres in the World Series.

OCTOBER 27, 1999

New York sweeps Atlanta in the World Series.

OCTOBER 26, 2000

The Yankees beat the Mets for their third title in four years.

OCTOBER 13, 2001

Jeter makes "the Flip" in the ALDS against the Oakland Athletics.

MARCH 31, 2003

Jeter suffers a separated shoulder and misses 39 games.

JULY 1, 2004

Jeter is bloodied diving into the stands to catch a foul ball against Boston.

MAY 26, 2006

Jeter records his 2,000th career hit.

SEPTEMBER 11, 2009

Jeter becomes the Yankees' all-time hits leader.

NOVEMBER 4, 2009

Jeter wins his last World Series as a player.

SEPTEMBER 28, 2014

Jeter retires after 20 seasons, all spent with the Yankees.

GLOSSARY

CATALYST
A person or thing that precipitates an event.

CLOSER
A pitcher who comes in at the end of the game to secure a win for his team.

DISABLED LIST
A list of players who are not available for play because of an injury.

ERROR
A fielding mistake.

MINOR LEAGUE
A lower level of baseball where players work on improving their skills before they reach the major leagues.

PROMOTION
The action of raising someone to a higher position or rank.

SHORTSTOP
A fielder who is usually positioned in the infield between second and third base.

ONLINE RESOURCES

To learn more about Derek Jeter and the New York Yankees, visit abdobooklinks.com. These links are routinely monitored and updated to provide the most current information available.

BOOKS

Dobrow, Larry, and Damien Jones. *Derek Jeter's Ultimate Baseball Guide 2015*. New York: Little Simon, 2015.

Herman, Gail. *Who Is Derek Jeter?* New York: Grosset & Dunlap, 2015.

Howell, Brian. *New York Yankees*. Minneapolis, MN: Abdo Publishing, 2015.

INDEX

ABOUT THE AUTHOR

Todd Karpovich is an award-winning writer based in Baltimore, Maryland. He has written for ESPN.com, the Associated Press, MLB.com, Sports Xchange, the *Baltimore Sun*, and other national media outlets. He is the coauthor of *Skipper Supreme: Buck Showalter and the Baltimore Orioles*.